HOW TO COMMUNICATE WITH CONFIDENCE
(Guidelines for expressing your confidence and speaking clearly)

DIANA VALENCIA

Table of contents

CHAPTER 1: How does behavioural economics transform communication?

CHAPTER 2: How to get more done with less effort by convincing others to support you.

CHAPTER 3: What is availability bias? - How to make people routinely, predictably, and dependably overweigh your viewpoint by triggering the availability bias

CHAPTER 4: What is anchoring effect in psychology? - How to charge more or pay less (for the same goods) and achieve quick influence using anchoring effect?

CHAPTER 5: What is cognitive bias?

CHAPTER 6: How Can You Use a Bias in Communication?

CHAPTER 1

How does behavioural economics transform communication?

"Behavioural economics is a fast emerging area of research anchored on psychology, economics and behavioural sciences. A motivating element behind the emergence of behavioural economics has been its recent application to habits that influence health."

Behavioural economics - which uses insights from psychology, sociology and increasingly neuroscience to explain people's decisions that traditional economic theory can't - provides new ways to think about the barriers and drivers to a range of behaviours, such as health insurance take-up and the tendency to contribute to retirement savings.

Article on behavioural economics (BE) by the administrators of the Johns Hopkins Centre for Communication Programs (CCP) gives examples from CCP social and behaviour change communication (SBCC) programmes to illustrate how BE concepts can aid the understanding of how people think, decide and act as they make choices that affect their health and the health of their families and communities.

1. "Framing (and a corollary, priming) refers to defining a decision scenario in a way that implies how an audience should think about it. The frame that is provided first primes the audience to think about the issue via that frame or lens rather than some other perspective.... The language used to convey a collection of alternatives can impact people's decision-making. People make default ('gut' reaction, rapid) judgments and might be more driven by emotional messages with immediate reward."

The example of framing is the Communication for Healthy Living (CHL)'s Mabrouk campaign in Egypt. (See related summary) Contraceptive usage, a main behavioural target, was positioned within a cycle of family health behaviours with celebrating marriage (Mabrouk!-Congratulations!) as the entrance point for the communication approach. The branded theme was designed to create a mind-set ("your health is your wealth") with messaging focused on benefits of "life stage" behaviours, including, for example:

I. Longer birth spacing resulting in better maternal and child health.
II. Immunization and breastfeeding improving the mental and physical development of infants.
III. Avoidance of second-hand smoke reducing cardiovascular disease and cancer risk.

2) Promise devices/Reminders are stuff "(like messages or SMSs) that remind us of a commitment we make. Behavioural economics proposes that humans make judgments naturally, by adopting mental shortcuts.

Commitment devices and reminders can assist lessen the cognitive effort necessary to sequence or complete a difficult job. Pre-committing to a certain option might help people align their behaviours with their preferences."

The example of this method is Tanzania Capacity and Communication Project's Wazazi Nipendeni SMS campaign (See linked summary) (See related summaries). This countrywide safe motherhood SBCC campaign is from CCP in conjunction with Media for Development International (MFDI) and the Tanzania Communication and Development Centre (TCDC) (TCDC). "All Wazazi Nipendeni media urges listeners and viewers to submit a free text message to a special short-message-service (SMS) number to obtain further information about safe pregnancy." Introductory questions are supplied for registration of pregnant women and moms to identify the date of pregnancy and deliver 3-4 scheduled information, recommendations, and reminders per week. From 2012 to 2016, 1,507,828 people had registered.

3)"A heuristic is a mental script or guide that facilitates decision-making or judgements. These rule-of-thumb tactics decrease decision-making time and allow individuals to perform without continually stopping to think about their next line of action. One way that communication might alter heuristics is via modelling behaviour so that individuals can have a mental image of how to do something without having to think about it. "

The Suaahara integrated nutrition project led by Save the Children and supported by CCP provided the Bhanchhin Aama ("Mother says") communication platform and campaign integrating SBCC messages and activities about nutrition with hygiene/sanitation, agriculture and health services promotion at all levels. The ad concentrated on the positive mother-in-law 'Bhanchhin Aama' who showed how to be a helpful mother-in-law through scripts that inspired family members to assist their pregnant women and moms.

4) " Behavioural defaults refers to what some study terms a "nudge," a small modification in a setting that makes one decision more likely than another....

A default is the option an individual will receive if he or she does not make an active decision. In behavioural economics, the default is generally something that an external organization such as a government agency or enterprise has imposed in order to maximize (optimally) the welfare of the group. The system is built so that the individual will automatically receive the default until they 'opt out'. For example, nations, whose default is that individuals will be organ donors, albeit they can 'opt out', have significantly greater rates of organ donation than other countries."

How does behavioural economics vary from traditional economics?

Furthermore, while increased informational efforts may help people quit, they could expand the gap between the smoking rates of better-educated and less-educated segments of society.

According to Professor Isoni, the reason why behavioural economics is now being hailed as a revolution is because we have grown accustomed to thinking of economics as being based on axioms of rational choice that are abstract in nature and whose psychological plausibility was largely uncontested for the majority of the previous century. In this regard, I am more inclined to think of it as a counter-revolution that returns economics to its foundations in psychological intuition and introspection (as in the writings of Adam Smith, the father of modern economics), with the difference that psychology is now recognized as a scientific discipline and can provide us with much more than intuitions and introspection.

The endowment effect, one of Thaler's biggest contributions, was expanded upon by Isoni's work with WBS colleague and Professor of Behavioural Science Graham Loomes.

We value things much more once they become a part of our endowment, or once we acquire them, because of our disproportionate distaste of losses, or what Kahneman and Tversky refer to as "loss aversion," says Isoni.

The endowment effect, which calls into question some of economics' most fundamental premises like the reversibility of indifference curves, has garnered a lot of attention. It also calls into question some significant findings like the Coase theorem, which asserts that when there are no transactions costs, people will naturally gravitate toward the most efficient and mutually beneficial outcome.

How Behavioural Economics Can Be Used to Enhance Daily Life

The study of behavioural economics gives light on many aspects of daily life, including why we choose to make particular decisions about ourselves or other people or how to proceed. It is an amazing lens that reveals our own biases and decision-making processes. It's one where we can better comprehend the constraints, drivers, origins, and bounds of our choices and actions—are it risk, resource allocation, strategic dependency, or irrationality. Microeconomic theory, social intelligence, neurology, and psychology have been combined to create a field that offers explanations for our relationships and influences how we behave on a daily basis.

State-dependent preferences:

Short-term preference changes, such as hunger, mood, or temperature, fall under this category. We underappreciate our changes in state-dependent preferences and are not very good at anticipating or accepting these changes.

When you go to the grocery store when you're hungry, for instance, you may project your feelings of hunger onto your purchases, believing erroneously that you won't be as hungry, irritable, or in the mood for sweets or unhealthy foods later (when you're at home and have eaten a meal, for instance). As a result, you may buy more items that you would find unappealing or expensive if you weren't as hungry. The projection bias is what's known as this. We may avoid the projection bias and make the most "ideal" decisions regardless of our present situation by being aware of our current situation. This can be anything from choosing to go grocery shopping while hungry to choosing to smoke cigarettes while considering the repercussions to choosing to interact socially while feeling agitated or unhappy, etc.

Receiving new information:

We constantly receive fresh textual and sensory information on a daily basis. Our propensity to view ambiguous facts as supporting our initial preferred theory is known as the confirmation bias. This is especially important for teachers who have preconceived notions about their pupils and interpret their behaviour in a way that fits that perception. This makes logical given that the heuristics and biases method describes how people use snap judgments to evaluate the likelihood of specific people, which can speed up cognitive processes but are vulnerable to biases that may be harmful.

Another is availability heuristics, where people judge the likelihood or frequency of events based on how easily they can be remembered. This explains why some people believe there will be more suicides than homicides, despite the fact that the data show the contrary, or why some people believe there will be more deaths from tornadoes and hurricanes than from vehicle accidents.

Deciding to change from a default:

One of the most significant phenomena that behavioural economists have researched is default effects. It is in line with nave hyperbolic discounting (where individuals make decisions only in the current period without correctly predicting the future and our preferences then).

They appear because of commission-omission biases (individuals care more about errors in commission than they do omission), loss aversion (so that individuals are affected by losses more than they are by the same-sized gains), the assumption that the default indicates what we should do, and the fact that we are unsure of how simple it is to switch. One of the most well-known instances is when the DMV changed the opt-in organ donation system from 30–40% donors to 70–80% donors, with the option for individuals to still choose not to donate their organs.

Gambling/Betting:

Another illustration would be if you were investing in stocks, insurance, or gambling. The Law of Tiny Numbers, which describes how people who see a small sample of events believe those events are representative of the underlying probabilities of those events, is a typical phenomenon in behavioural economics. This leads to the Gambler's Fallacy, which is the misconception that a result that hasn't happened in a while is more likely to happen in a series of independent draws from a distribution. For instance, if you are playing roulette and the ball has come up red four times in a row, you might believe that the ball will come up black next even if each has a separate probability of being either a black or a red. Therefore, being aware of this myth could increase your gambling success. The hot-hand fallacy, on the other hand (though still connected to the Law of Small Numbers), describes how individuals tend to make predictions based on recent events or a small sample size rather than the underlying probability when a player plays several successful shots in a row.

Insurance and stocks:

People frequently overestimate minor possibilities while purchasing insurance, which results in excessive premium costs. For instance, Cicchetti and Dubin (1994) investigated why customers choose to get insurance to protect their telephone wiring. Customers had the option of paying the $60 repair cost upfront or purchasing insurance for $0.45/month. According to estimates from the phone provider, wire damage will cost $0.26; therefore consumers are paying a 100% premium for insurance. The neoclassical anticipated utility theory is incompatible with this clear aversion to small-scale hazards. In terms of stocks, one behavioural economic discovery is that some people hold the Belief of Mean Reversion, or the notion that stocks will eventually return to their previous prices. Because of this, many people hang onto "losing" stocks and sell "winners," regardless of the sustainability of those stocks on the stock market.

CHAPTER 2

How to get more done with less effort by convincing others to support you

Persuasion is primarily about communication at its core. But the art of persuasion involves employing a complex combination of leadership and communication skills to win others over to your ideas, suggestions, or proposals after—and only after—you've effectively persuaded them that doing so will be in their best interests.

In particular for transformative leaders, the capacity to persuade others has long been a top leadership and communication talent, and the rate of technical, human capital, and workforce change has further accelerated the demand. If you lack the ability to convince and influence others, can you still be a successful change agent? If you are unable to engage people in your vision or successfully assist them in embracing a new procedure, system, or approach, can you still motivate them to take action? If you don't understand influence and how to utilize it to persuade people to accept your views, how can you lead anything or anyone at all?

While persuasion is about persuading people to change their minds, it is also about selling or presenting your views. You should be acutely aware of the kinds of questions that people begin asking the moment you start talking to them if you want to maximize the possibility that your suggestions, recommendations, and proposals will be accepted—and implemented. You should always speak and act in a way that serves the needs and interests of the people you are seeking to influence. You will be better able to determine needs and interests and persuade others to act on your brilliant ideas if you adhere to these five procedures. You can successfully use the art of persuasion with the aid of these five stages.

1. Make people want to pay attention to you.

People who refuse to listen to you are impossible to persuade. When you approach your audience with a fresh idea, advice, or proposition, one of the first things they'll consider is if they should even give you the time of day. They'll undoubtedly wonder if they should even pay attention to you.

Everyone is occupied. You may assume that people aren't trying to waste your time with ideas they don't think or know they need because they barely have time to exercise, eat, or spend quality time with their friends and family. It is essential that you can rapidly explain to them why and how what you have to say matters. You must first persuade someone to give you some time and listen to you before you can convince them to do anything.

You won't ever be able to convince your audience to care about anything else on the subject if you don't make it apparent how your message (whatever it is) relates to their lives, workplaces, or organizations.

2. Demonstrate your genuine concern for others by attending to their needs.

People will continue to wonder why they should care about the issue even after they choose to start paying attention to you. They will be expressing internal complaints that are completely unrelated to whatever eye contact or aggressive listening you may have observed.

Don't be tricked into believing you can skip this step if you haven't yet worked to make sure they know you care.

You must make sure they can tell that you care after you have their attention. Start paying attention to the people you wish to influence; this is the finest method to demonstrate your concern. You need to comprehend people's difficulties, problems, pain areas, etc. if you want to persuade them. The next step is to ask deliberative, open-ended questions that serve to broaden the conversation to a subject relevant to your goals.

When listeners begin to sense and trust that you care, you'll know because they'll start sharing more. Your audience will undoubtedly let you know where they want to go if you listen carefully. And if you are very effective at leading with influence, they will actually allow you to lead them in the direction you want. Naturally, there must be a shared interest as well as obvious similarities between where they think they want to go and where you intend to take them, or a justification for the differences.

The main lesson to be learned from this is that before you can ever hope for your audience to care about your requirements, you must first consider theirs.
You won't even need to worry about the next step if you don't show that you care by being aware of and responsive to their wants and interests because they won't ever be able to trust you.

3. Give others a reason to believe you.

People will begin considering if they can trust you once they sense that you care. But for them, it will go further. Your audience will be debating whether or not to believe you internally as you read this. People must feel at ease working with you and with the way you conduct yourself in front of them. To determine whether they should trust you and, even then, how much, they will look for internal and external endorsements, validators, or other forms of confirmation.

So who are you? How do people perceive you? What support do you have for your claims? How do you become an expert? It is your obligation to enter the room aware that your audience is thinking up a lot of questions about you; after all, they might never come right out and ask any of them. You should be aware that there is an association between influence and trust, as well as between influence and persuasion. The more credibility and confidence your audience has in you, the more likely it is that they will be open to your ideas and actually consider them. Building trust is the best way to overcome opposition to novel or unconventional ideas.

Don't bother asking your audience to change their behaviour, support your cause, or adopt or implement your ideas or plans if you can't first establish their trust. You will have been silenced inwardly by them. They might still be talking to you, but if you don't establish their trust, you'll miss the chance to engage them and fully explain your points.

4. Give your arguments in terms of advantages and disadvantages that will appeal to your audience.

If your audience has listened to you this far, you are doing pretty well since it shows that they are paying attention to you. They have decided to give you and your message a high degree of legitimacy and trust because they think you care. But don't risk missing this opportunity. You still have some significant work to perform, so proceed when the situation and timing are appropriate.

Your big ideas, suggestions, or proposals will really come into play here. To convince somebody to act differently, you must provide evidence in this situation. Here is where you can really show how much you care about the wants and desires of your audience. Here, you'll match those demands or difficulties with approaches that further their objectives or address their issues. Your audience will nevertheless be perplexed as to why they should make any move at all. There will still be some remaining concerns even if they agree with what you are proposing and your new ideas.

Describe how your suggestions will directly help the person, the team, or the business to allay those last concerns. In addition to outlining the advantages and disadvantages of everything, you should explain why they should act (change something; do something different). The WIIFM and the WIIFO are where it begins and ends. People need to know "what's in it for me" and "what's in it for my organization," so you must explain both.

Your audience won't act if they don't believe in the advantages and gains that they, they, or their organizations will enjoy if they implement your suggestions. In a similar vein, they won't act if they don't fully understand the repercussions of inaction. Use this opportunity to properly explain your suggestions, support your thoughts, and provide an explanation for your opinions. If you do this well enough, people will probably take action.

5. Clarify the process and the action phases.

Having been inspired to act, your audience needs your assistance in understanding the course of action and method they will follow. Your target audience is prepared to accept your ideas, suggestions, or proposals at this stage of the persuasive process, but they are unsure of the next stages and the procedure. Without a plan of action, you cannot abandon them.

The true goal of the art of persuasion is to change people's behaviour or motivate them to take action, not only to sell an idea. Don't leave folks with no clear instructions on how to achieve fresh and different results.

You can lessen uncertainty and dread by clarifying the next steps. Additionally, when a procedure is clearly outlined, perceived risks are reduced.

Your entire work will be in vain if you don't outline the specific actions to take or make the process clear. The audience might have enjoyed what you said and even how you said it, but without a plan of action, they won't act on it. After convincing someone to act differently, you ought to assist them with comprehending how to do so.

The key points...

Everyone who wants to bring about change and persuade others to act can benefit from using this five-step needs assessment and persuasion technique. It is not a method of manipulation. You need to learn how to persuade people, whether you're a job applicant trying to convince the hiring manager to hire you, a manager of sales trying to implement new communication strategies, a change lead in charge of persuading colleagues about the advantages of your next digital transformation initiative, an HR executive in charge of a thorough work-design overhaul, or a marketing executive leading a new approach to performance.

This point merits reiteration. While persuasion is about persuading people to change their minds, it is also about selling or presenting your views. It is your obligation to anticipate the kinds of inquiries that will enter your listeners' minds as soon as you begin speaking with them. You run the risk of failing if you proceed with your presentation, sales pitch, or proposal without taking your audience's demands into account. You have a far better chance of success if you proceed and base your presentation and recommendations on the aforementioned five-step needs assessment and persuasive approach.

Simple Strategies for Getting Anyone To Do Anything

Have you ever encountered someone who was able to manipulate you? I do, and I've always yearned for this elusive talent.

Numerous publications and academic programs assert to have the answers to persuasion. Although they are excellent resources for learning how to persuade, they frequently overcomplicate the subject and neglect tried-and-true strategies for effective interpersonal communication.

Being more persuasive doesn't require you to be a brilliant salesperson with boundless confidence. Simply paying closer attention to the fundamentals will increase your chances of success.

1. Make your language impactful.

The pitch itself must be loaded with language that genuinely prompts a reaction. By structuring your statements around essential phrases, you can achieve this goal quickly.

For instance, the term "auto accident" conjures up images of numerous different car wrecks. However, you wouldn't claim that there are thousands of automobile accidents every day if you were attempting to get someone to purchase auto insurance. You'll claim that thousands of people lose their lives in auto accidents every day.

The phrase "death" is more potent than "accident," and advertisers employ this tactic daily to persuade consumers to purchase goods.

2. Don't act haughty, but dress nice.

Even if no one is there to see you, wearing nice clothes can help you stay confident. Being the best-dressed person in the room might have the unfortunate side effect of making you talk down to or act in a condescending manner toward those who are genuinely above you.

This is a simple trap to slip into since we are more inclined to patronize the other person if we feel like we are in control of the conversation by saying things like, "Oh, well, let me explain this to you. It's actually fairly easy. The issue is that you've very much lost them if it's complicated or if you're not speaking clearly. Remember that the person you are making a pitch to is superior to you. They have the authority to refuse.

Talking down to the individual is challenging them to a contest you don't want to enter, but you certainly don't want them to recognize this since you need to remain in control of the conversation. Keep in mind that there is a thin line between being forceful and being cocky.

3. Think about the future.

A fantastic technique to convey confidence is to use the future tense. It helps the other person see that you are making progress and are prepared to keep your word.

Abusing the word "will" will make this simple for you. The person will become accustomed to the concept that this is going to happen if you use words like "We will" and "Then we'll do this."

However, avoid becoming pushy. Try to avoid making decisions for the other person and instead discuss the options and possible outcomes.

4. Make yourself scarce.

What people can't have, they want. Make it apparent that they will miss out on this opportunity because this offer you are making to them is temporary.

This is especially effective if you are selling something. Making new products purposefully rare and hard to get is a common strategy for selling them off since it encourages consumers to "Get it now while you can!"

5. Select the appropriate platform for your pitch.

You're attempting to persuade someone to carry out an action they probably don't want to (yet). This means that creating a positive atmosphere for your pitch is really important.

Discover the person's preferred communication style by doing some research. As long as you give them some options, simply asking someone if they prefer phone calls over emails can go a long way.

Even some folks I've encountered prefer texting to face-to-face communication. Remember this and select a media that is focused on them rather than you.

6. Speak their language.

Its terrible manners to continue someone else's statement. This is due to the fact that you are interjecting your own "talk" into their free-standing ideas.

Who desires to feel oppressed?
Pay close attention to the way the speaker speaks and observe their demeanour. Select your own strategy accordingly. Do they veer off the jargon? And you ought to. Do they crack jokes and use prepositions to complete their sentences? Incorporate your own laid-back manner into that.

Effective body language should be matched. When someone prefers to communicate actively, as is the case when they like to converse with their hands, it is beneficial for you to follow suit. If their body language is restrained and closed off (closed arms, etc.), you know to steer clear of gestures that can make them uneasy.

Additionally, this method works effectively when speaking to crowds of people. Get a sense of the atmosphere in the space by observing what makes others respond favourably to your words. Discover what works and use it appropriately.

7. Abstain from superfluous words.

You lose respect from the person you're speaking to every time you allow "um" or "uh" to interrupt. Even the fact that what you have to say is significant won't matter.

Let your speech flow while being clear. The most effective approach to achieve this is to practice speaking at home or to pause before speaking.

8. Take action to help them.

When you were a child, you undoubtedly greeted your parents with a kind word before requesting something. We learn even as children that asking for a favour in return increases the likelihood that someone will assist us.

Before even making a pitch, you can do this. When you start a networking relationship by doing someone a favour, they are more inclined to cooperate with you in the future.

You ought to do the same in return because you never know what might be noted about you. I once gave this site an uninvited favour by recommending a fantastic website. The person who received this favour was so appreciative of the increase in sales that they provided me free goods. Although neither they nor I asked for it, its establishment solidified a bond that might later result in more mutually beneficial outcomes.

9. Become an expert at timing.

This is related to getting to know the target audience for your proposal. Find the optimum time to speak with them by studying them.

For instance, some busy executives start the week overwhelmed and mentally check out on Friday. This suggests that the best day to approach someone you need to convince may be Thursday.

If you're trying to convince a friend or family member, it will be simpler because you know them better. Choose

the appropriate time to approach them, and your chances
of success will soar.

10. Say what you think, but grudgingly.

You desire the confidence of the other person. You know
the solutions, but how did you arrive at them?

Talk about your previous beliefs and your current beliefs.
Use your personal learning experience as an example for
them to follow. By doing this, you are controlling the
pace of the conversation or pitch and assuring the person
that this will be beneficial to them.

11. Reiterate their words.

Show that you are paying attention to and
acknowledging the other person's thoughts and feelings.
If I understand you correctly, you're suggesting that you
find this significant because of XY and Z. Can you
please confirm my understanding? I recognize that and
believe AB and C.

I assure you that this is useful even if you are not dealing
with the alphabet.

12. Amplify your feelings.

Allow your feelings, such as joy and excitement, to emerge naturally throughout the talk. Avoid infusing the person with zeal they don't yet feel.

In many circumstances, you'll want to save your most passionate and emotional remarks until the end of your pitch. This will guarantee that it conveys sincerity and is rationally supported by what has already been said.

As a general guideline, get the conversations going on a positive yet laid-back note. Increase your level of enthusiasm and excitement for the subject at hand as you begin the conversation. The person won't sense that they are being "worked" in this way. Instead, they'll think you're helping them out.

How does marketing employ behavioural economics?

The field of behavioural economics investigates how variables that don't directly relate to the product itself can have an impact on a customer's decision to buy. Psychological, cognitive, emotional, cultural, or social elements can be among these.

The main goal of marketing is to persuade customers to choose your company over a rival.

Understanding how customer decisions can be influenced by behavioural economics helps marketing efforts.

Therefore, even minor adjustments to the product, branding, or menu of options can have a significant impact on how customers behave.

Let's examine the nine outstanding applications of behavioural economics in marketing.

Principle No. 1 of behavioural economics: The power of FREE

Free is one of the most effective marketing buzzwords there is.

Because of this, supermarkets will often advertise "Buy One, Get One Free," rather than "Buy Two Products, Get 50% Off."

Although the core of each of these offers is the same, customers will get a beautiful dopamine rush when they see the term "Free," and this will be reinforced if they take advantage of that offer.

Typical marketing illustration: Subway

While many companies no longer provide such promotions because consumers can see through the gimmick, certain companies, like Subway, still offer "Buy one, get one free" specials in order to draw people in on occasions like World Sandwich Day.

The second behavioural economics tenet is social proof.

One of the most effective behavioural economics strategies, particularly in online marketing, is social proof. It is a propensity to be influenced by other people's decisions, especially in hazy situations.

People are more likely to purchase well-known goods or services in order to gain respect from their peers, which is why so many customers read online reviews in order to determine how reliable a business is. In fact, 81% of customers believe that a business with many positive reviews is trustworthy.

Typical marketing example: UK government

The commercial sector is not the only one that influences individuals to perform the desired action using behavioural economics principles.
Here is an illustration of how the UK government applied the social proof theory to promote organ donation.

Even if a customer is visiting a brand for the first time, social evidence increases their level of trust in the business.

Scarcity is the third behavioural economics premise.

The power of scarcity in behavioural economics is something you already understand if you're familiar with limited-edition products.

Simply put, people tend to place more value on a product if they believe there is a limited supply or a short window of time within which they can purchase it before it sells out.

Typical marketing illustration: Starbucks

Starbucks is a marketing guru when it comes to scarcity. We are all aware of the buzz around Pumpkin Spice Lattes, and one of the key factors is that they are only offered for a limited time each year.

The promotion for these goods revolves around the phrase "Enjoy it while it lasts," and the coffee giant routinely introduces limited-edition seasonal foods and beverages.

Principle #4 of behavioural economics: Loss aversion

People are more terrified of losing what they already have than of gaining something new.
This basically indicates that we are significantly more likely to feel regret when we lose money than we are to feel delight when we win it.

According to the loss aversion principle, in order to convince a customer of a product's benefits, we must emphasize what they stand to lose if they decide against making a purchase.

An example of marketing in action is Amazon Lightning Deals.

Amazon's daily Lightning Deals are the clearest illustration of loss aversion. These are the limited-time, reduced deals that can only be used by a specific number of customers and are only valid for 24 hours or less.

Due to this restriction, this specials page is prominently displayed on the website, enticing customers to act swiftly to prevent "losing out."

Fifth behavioural economics principle: Shareholding

Almost all popular online membership businesses provide free trials.

By granting customers a free trial, you're fostering a sense of ownership over the good or service, which fosters an emotional bond.

Consumers are given the option of losing the product after the trial period or paying to continue the service.

Netflix is a common illustration in marketing.

You'd think that offering a 30-day free trial to potential Netflix customers to test the service out would be a significant loss-maker for the firm, but the contrary is actually true.

Principle #6 of behavioural economics: Framing

Framing, very simply, is presenting features of your product in a way that appeals to customers' emotions.

Typical marketing illustration: Tesla

In this excellent Tesla illustration, the advertisements are framed to emphasize the features of the car that make it a distinctive product.

Tesla uses certain characteristics (such how the car's powertrain is silent) to emphasize how distinctive the product is, knowing that the customer is already aware of their brand and product.

It's a straightforward message, yet it contributes to the consumer's conception that this product will make them stand out from other car owners.

Rule #7 of behavioural economics: Dominated alternative/Third Decoy

The Dominated Alternative (or Third Decoy) principle demonstrates how the introduction of a third, less appealing option can affect the decision that customers make.

Typical marketing illustration: Shutter stock

Shutter stock offers four different subscription plans at various price rates. The pre-selected one costs £99 per month for 350 photos, or 28p each.

The less priced options in this illustration seem to be a ruse to make the more expensive subscriptions seem like a better deal.

Since the cheapest option costs £19 per month for 10 photographs, which works out to £1.90 per image, the consumer feels justified in purchasing a more expensive membership since they believe they are receiving a better value.

The decision paradox is principle no. 8 of behavioural economics.

More options don't always translate into higher sales, and analysis paralysis is a serious problem.
More options frequently result in consumers feeling overwhelmed, leaving without buying, or delaying purchases out of concern over making the wrong choice.

Typical marketing illustration: Site Ground

When consumers first set up their hosting service, Site Ground provides them with three alternatives, similar to many other software-as-a-service companies. However, after a customer is set up, add-on purchases and other services like managed transfers, SSL certificates, and more are made available to them.

This tactic boosts sales and lessens decision fatigue.

Principle #9 of behavioural economics: Anchoring

You will begin to notice the anchoring principle everywhere once you are aware of it.
Giving clients the most expensive option initially in order to make all subsequent selections appear more affordable is known as anchoring.

Typical marketing illustration: Crazy Egg

The subscription choices for Crazy Egg's **heat map** tracking program are a prime illustration of this. Customers are more likely to select the "Pro" plan because it is listed first on the left. This plan, which costs

$99, serves as the standard by which all other plans are measured.

Additionally, you'll see that this illustration makes use of a number of other behavioural economic principles, like framing (highlighting the "Plus plan" in a different colour to capture the eye) and the decoy effect (providing cheaper, but less desirable, options).

Behavioural economics is crucial to marketing.

If you want to find quick fixes for commercial success, it is crucial to understand how behavioural economics principles are applied in marketing.

Marketing professionals may learn more about the human mind and use empirical data on how people make decisions thanks to behavioural economics.

CHAPTER 3

What is availability bias?

The availability bias refers to the propensity for people to believe that instances of things that immediately come to mind are more representative than they actually are. One of several cognitive biases that impair critical thinking and, as a result, the reliability of our decisions is the psychological phenomena.

The availability heuristic, which is described as relying on the first things that come to mind in order to make snap decisions and judgments, is the source of the availability bias. That reliance lessens the need for time-consuming fact-checking and research but raises the possibility that our choices will be erroneous.

It stands to reason that the things that stand out the most are the easiest to recall. How effectively we recall things are affected by a variety of factors, though. For instance, it's easier for us to recall things that we personally seen than those that we merely heard about. Therefore, even though we have read statistics to the contrary, we are inclined to overestimate the percentage of businesses that succeed if, for instance, we personally know of numerous start-ups and they are all successful.

Similar to how people recall intense experiences like car accidents and lottery winnings, some of us tend to overestimate the likelihood that our car would crash or, more naively but equally mistaken, that we will win the jackpot. The availability bias in these situations causes some people to avoid flying at all costs and other people to depend on a significant lottery win as a retirement plan.

Other cognitive biases include the self-serving bias, which entails putting a good spin on our own actions and interpreting confusing evidence in a way that suits our own interests, and the confirmation bias, which is giving undue attention to materials that support our own views and attitudes.

Humans are prone to a variety of errors, including cognitive biases. One of the first steps in developing our capacity for critical thought is becoming aware of our propensity to do such errors.

How to make people routinely, predictably, and dependably overweigh your viewpoint by triggering the availability bias

"The attention we give to an event is proportionate to how vivid or exciting it is, and it is a well-known fact that, other things being equal, what fascinates us most at the moment is also what we remember best."
--James, William

The availability heuristic explains why receiving one award increases your chances of receiving another. It explains why we occasionally refrain from doing something out of fear and instead choose to take a riskier action. It explains why governments shell out astronomical sums of money to reduce threats we've already encountered. It explains why your worldview is significantly influenced by the five individuals closest to you. It explains why a ton of evidence showing something is bad doesn't always persuade people to stay away from it. This explains why a rising stock market might give the impression that everything is going fine.

And it explains how negative publicity can ultimately be advantageous.

Here is how the availability heuristic functions, how to go around it, and how to take advantage of it.

What is availability in psychology?

Which profession—police officer or logger—is riskier? Despite the fact that high-profile police shootings may have made you believe otherwise, studies suggest that loggers are more likely than police officers to perish while working.

Our brains use a variety of different techniques to generate snap judgments about relative risk or danger when it comes to making these kinds of decisions. This exemplifies the availability heuristic, a mental shortcut that facilitates quick but occasionally inaccurate judgments.

There are many different types of mental shortcuts, but one popular one is to rely on knowledge that is remembered rapidly. This is what "availability" means.

You'll think something is more common if you can think of several instances of it happening right away, like police shootings.

Workings of the availability heuristic

Let's quickly review the field from where the availability heuristic originates before we describe it.

The study of behavioural economics combines insights from psychology and economics to show how actual people behave in the real world. This is in contrast to the conventional economic theory of human nature, which presupposed that people always act in a way that is consistent with their rational and stable interests. Amos Tversky and Daniel Kahneman's research, two psychologists, helped to launch the area in major part in the 1960s and 1970s.

According to the theory of behavioural economics, people frequently make decisions and judgements in the face of uncertainty by employing faulty heuristics rather than by carefully evaluating all the pertinent factors. We can make decisions quickly by using quick heuristics rather of spending the time and mental energy to consider all the options.

They typically result in positive effects. They may, however, influence us to make decisions that are constantly irrational and go against what economics would suggest is the best option. Heuristics are often used without our awareness, and even when we deliberately try to be more rational, it is difficult to change them.

The availability heuristic, initially researched by Tversky and Kahneman in 1973, is one such cognitive shortcut. We frequently evaluate the possibility and importance of events based on how quickly they flash into our minds. A piece of information appears more significant to us the more "accessible" it is to us. As a result, we place more importance on material that we have just learned because it is simpler to recall a current news piece than a science lecture from years ago. To attempt to search through every piece of knowledge that might be in our heads would be excessively laborious.

We also give information that is surprising or unusual more weight. We underestimate the likelihood of shark attacks and plane crashes because they are more common than unintentional drowning or auto accidents. It will be simpler for us to recall if a group of similar items is placed beside one unique one. For instance, the "9" would be the character that is most likely to be recalled from the string of letters "RTASDT9RTGS" since it sticks out from the other letters.

According to Timur Kuran and Cass Sunstein's article in Behavioural Law and Economics:

"Other recent examples include the widespread protests against Agent Orange, asbestos in schools, breast implants, and child-endangering airbags in automobiles. Their commonality is that individuals tended to base their risk assessments primarily—if not entirely—on data generated through social processes as opposed to through personal experience or independent research. A public upheaval happened in each instance as a large number of participants responded to one another's deeds and words. Additionally, in each case, the need for quick, extensive, and expensive government intervention became seen as morally imperative and socially desirable—despite the fact that, in most or all instances, the restrictions that resulted may have done more harm than good.

More people remember stories than random data. Fables, fairy tales, myths, proverbs, and stories are used by cultures all over the world to impart valuable life lessons and morals.

Information can also become more relevant through personal experience. If you've just been in a car accident, you might now see car accidents as being more frequent than they were previously. The base rates are still the same; all that has changed is that every time you get in a car, a bad, fresh memory comes to mind. We tend to dismiss occurrences that aren't immediately remembered since we take our memories for granted as representative and truthful. Another illustration might be that after experiencing the effects of a natural disaster, you could be more inclined to get insurance against future occurrences.

Anything that makes something simpler to recall has a bigger effect on us. In a previous study, Tversky and Kahneman asked participants if they thought it was more likely for a random English word to start with "K" or have "K" as the third letter. People tended to believe the former was more often since it is usually simpler to remember terms that start with a particular letter. Contrarily, this is real.

What deceives us about the availability heuristic?

People "tend to appraise the relative importance of topics by the ease with which they are retrieved from memory—and this is greatly influenced by the scope of media coverage."

Going back to the reasons expressed in the opening of this essay, winning an award can increase your chances of winning another award since it increases your visibility and makes it easier for others to associate your name with that kind of honour. Sometimes, because the risks of the latter are more memorable, we choose to avoid something else in favour of something that is objectively riskier, such as driving rather than flying.

Your perspective might be significantly influenced by the five individuals closest to you because you constantly come into contact with them and are reminded of them when you form your own beliefs. Despite mountains of evidence to the contrary, people aren't always persuaded to stay away from something if the risks aren't immediately apparent to them, for example, if they haven't directly seen them. When the stock market is rising, it can appear that everything is going well because it is a straightforward, obvious, and hence remembered indicator. In the long run, negative publicity can be advantageous if it increases the likelihood that people will remember something, like a contentious book, by causing it to be frequently cited.
In the absence of mitigating circumstances, these are the logical consequences of the availability heuristic rather than empirical principles.

We are what we remember, and how we see the world is greatly influenced by our memories. A number of things affect what we ultimately recall, including the following:

Our underlying assumptions about the world; our expectations

The following factors influence how we feel about information: how often we are exposed to it, how it makes us feel, and where it came from.

The likelihood of something occurring and how remembered it is are not really related. The contrary is frequently true, in fact. Unusual incidents draw more attention and stick out than regular ones. The availability heuristic as a result skews our perception of hazards in two significant ways:

We overestimate the probability of improbable events. Additionally, we overestimate the probability of plausible outcomes.

Overestimating the likelihood of unexpected events causes us to worry excessively, keeping us awake at night and eventually making our hair grey. We risk squandering a great deal of time, money, and other resources trying to control issues that, overall, don't have much of an influence. Sometimes these mitigating measures backfire, and other times they give us an unwarranted sense of security.

On the other hand, we might overestimate our chances of experiencing exceptional good fortune. Looking at everyone's social media highlights can lead us to believe that our own life will similarly be a series of significant successes and delights. However, the majority of people lead normal lives, and the moments we witness are typically extraordinary rather than typical.

How do i overcome availability heuristic?

A cognitive bias is typically difficult to eradicate simply by being aware of it. Even experts in behavioural economics like Kahneman who have studied it for many years occasionally struggle with the same nonsensical patterns. However, being aware of the availability heuristic allows you to take a step back to ensure that it isn't clouding your judgment when you need to make a crucial decision. Here are five strategies for reducing the availability heuristic's impact.

#1. When assessing probability, base rates should always be taken into account.

The average prevalence of anything within a given population is its base rate. For instance, approximately 10% of people are left-handed. In the absence of additional pertinent information, you would be correct in assuming that 1 in 10 random people are left-handed.

When estimating the likelihood of something, try to look at the base rate.

#2. Observe patterns and trends.

We learn that severe events typically follow more moderate ones thanks to the mental model of regression to the mean. Outlier incidents frequently result from chance and karma. They're not always illuminating. Base your decisions whenever possible on trends and patterns—the longer-term, the better. Even though exceptional events are more memorable, track record is everything.

#3. Consider your options carefully before making a decision.

Heuristics are designed to reduce the time and effort required to analyse a large amount of data and form an opinion. However, as we frequently point out, smart decisions require careful thought. There is no quick fix for that. The only way to avoid using the availability heuristic while making critical decisions is to take a moment to review the pertinent data rather than assuming whatever comes to mind first is accurate.

#4. Keep track of information that you might need to make a decision in the distant future.

Never depend on recollection. Annual performance reviews at work are used as an example by Max Bazerman and Don Moore in their book Judgment in Managerial Decision-Making. In contrast to the nine months before, managers frequently base their evaluations more on the most recent three months. It's far simpler than trying to recall everything that happened over the course of a year. Additionally, managers frequently overestimate the significance of unexpected one-off behaviour, such as a significant failure or success, without taking the larger pattern into account. In this situation, keeping track of observations about a person's performance throughout the course of the entire year would result in a more accurate evaluation.

#5. Go back and review earlier data.

Before making a decision, it's a good idea to review the pertinent facts in your memory even if you believe you can recall all that is significant.

We lack the energy to consider what is in front of us because we are too exhausted from thinking about improbable events. When it matters most, you won't be able to pay heed to such indications if you're frequently concerned and anxious.

This is not to imply you shouldn't be ready for the worst, though. Or that improbable events never occur (according to Littlewood's Law, a once-in-a-million event occurs at least once a month). We should be careful not to solely plan for the extremes as they are the ones that will stick in our memories.

CHAPTER 4

What is anchoring effect in psychology?

How to charge more or pay less (for the same goods) and archive quick influence – using anchoring effect

The anchoring effect is a cognitive bias that characterizes people's propensity to base their decisions unduly on the first piece of information they are given (the "anchor"). Anchoring happens when people base subsequent judgments on an initial piece of information during decision-making. Once an anchor is established, subsequent decisions are made by moving away from it, and there is a bias toward framing subsequent data in relation to the anchor. For instance, the initial offer price for a used car sets the bar for the rest of the discussions, making lower offers seem fairer even when they are still more than the car's actual value.

The anchoring effect frequently occurs in negotiations, although goal setting can influence the outcome.

Negotiation experts Deborah Zetik and Alice Stuhlmacher of DePaul University discovered that when negotiators set explicit, difficult goals, they consistently outperform those who set lower or vague goals in a study of goal-setting literature. Perhaps not unexpectedly, when negotiators receive benefits for achieving a goal, like a $10,000 bonus for billing 2,000 hours, performance goes up. But even a non-rewarding objective, like running five miles today, improves performance.

However, there may be a number of disadvantages to having high negotiation goals. Most clearly, not accomplishing your objective can make you less happy with the final result. Researchers Adam Galinsky, Victoria Medvec, and Thomas Mussweiler discovered in one study that high-achieving negotiators were less content with their results than their counterparts while having objectively better outcomes than peers who did not focus on high goals.

Notably, these high achievers' happiness correlated with quantitative measures of performance when they were asked to think about their reservation prices (walk-away points) and then evaluate their results. The takeaway? During the negotiation, keep your attention on your audacious aim to optimize your results. After the negotiation, compare your outcome to your reservation price to increase your happiness (or that of your supervisor).

You might have to decide between impasse and an undesirable alternative if you commit to your goal by restricting your future flexibility (for example, by publicly publicizing your commitment to a low purchasing price in advance). When dealing with people who are prone to making significant compromises under pressure and when building a reputation for toughness is crucial, aggressive commitment tactics are most effective.

Philadelphia had a $250 million annual budget shortfall and some of the highest paid municipal employees in the nation when Ed Rendell took office as mayor in 1992.

Rendell was aware that the labour unions could offer concessions, but that doing so would be challenging.

According to the New York Times, before talks ever began, Rendell publicly reaffirmed—almost daily—his commitment to balance the city's budget and, if necessary, tolerating a strike. He was able to commit to his difficult goal thanks to these words. Rendell presented a deal to union members that included, among other things, a 33-month wage freeze. After going on strike, the workers quickly accepted the offer. The agreement helped the city save an estimated $374 million over the following four years.

Last but not least, defining goals may increase motivation for bad actions like cheating. Researchers Maurice Schweitzer, Lisa Ordonez, and Bambi Douma show that failure to achieve goals increases the likelihood of people engaging in unethical activity, such as lying to claim success. Giving your sales team difficult goals could inspire them to log fraudulent sales in addition to legal ones.

How often do you exclaim, "Wow, that's pricey? I'm aware that the other store has far better prices. Or "Wow! Look at this fantastic discount! When buying goods and services, many buyers consider the value of a good deal. How do shoppers determine whether a product is a good deal? Shopping around for a good or service typically entails frequent reference to the costs, whether online or in a physical location. However, the first price a customer encounters is what they use as a standard reference point when shopping about. The anchoring effect refers to the propensity for people to base their decisions significantly on the initial piece of information they learn. An example of cognitive bias is the anchoring effect, which is a deliberate inaccuracy in judgment and decision-making. In judgments involving numerical values, such as prices, anchoring is important.

An example of a cognitive bias is anchoring.

Heuristics, or mental shortcuts, are frequently used by people while making choices. People frequently use the following heuristic while creating a budget, for instance: "I'll save 10% of my salary while I'm working so that I have emergency savings to pay for daily costs if I lose my job." Heuristics can speed up decision-making, but they can also result in cognitive biases that limit the information shoppers should take into account. Because people frequently rely on their first piece of information, the anchoring effect is a type of cognitive bias because it causes them to either make a decision too fast and neglect to search around for lower pricing or to ignore other information, such as the product's quality.

Heuristics known as price anchors give customers a simple and comfortable starting point. Because no one loves to constantly challenge themselves or make difficult decisions, anchoring is more enticing and powerful than one might initially believe.

How Decision Making Is Affected by Psychology's Anchoring Bias

People frequently utilize an anchor or focal point as a starting point or point of reference while trying to make a decision. People tend to depend excessively on the very first piece of information they learn, which can have a significant impact on the choice they ultimately make, according to psychologists. This particular cognitive bias is referred to as the anchoring bias or anchoring effect in psychology.

Amos Tversky and Daniel Kahneman wrote in a 1974 paper, "People make estimates by starting with an initial value that is altered to yield the final answer." "The problem's formulation may propose the initial value or starting point, or it may be the outcome of a partial computation. Adjustments are frequently insufficient in either situation. In other words, distinct estimates that are skewed toward the beginning values are produced from different starting locations."

Even arbitrary numbers, according to Tversky and Kahneman, might influence participants' estimations. In one instance, participants chose a number between 0 and 100 by spinning a wheel. The participants were then asked to increase or decrease that figure to represent the number of UN member states that were from Africa. In contrast to those who spun low numbers, those who spun high numbers provided greater estimates. The participants were making decisions in each instance based on that initial number as their anchor point.

Anchoring Bias Can Affect Your Price Comfort Level

Take the purchase of a new car, for instance. You discover that the average cost of the car you're considering is $27,000 online. When the dealer offers you the same vehicle at the nearby car lot for $26,500, you promptly accept it because it is $500 less than what you had anticipated paying. However, the car dealership across the street is selling the exact same vehicle for under $24,000, which is $3,000 less than the average price you discovered online and $2,500 less than what you spent.

You may later blame yourself for making such a hasty choice and not looking around for a better offer. So why did you accept the first offer so quickly?

According to the anchoring bias, we tend to favour the first piece of knowledge we encounter.

Since your initial research indicated that $27,000 was the average price, the first offer you encountered seemed like a great deal. You overlooked further information, such as the possibility that other dealers might have lower prices, and made a decision on the information you already had, which served as an anchoring point in your mind.

It Can Influence Your Salary Negotiations

Imagine that you are trying to negotiate a pay raise with your boss. You might hesitate to make an initial offer, but research suggests that being the first one to lay your cards down on the table might actually be the best way to go. Whoever makes that first offer has the edge since the anchoring effect will essentially make that number the starting point for all further negotiations. Not only that, it will bias those negotiations in your favor. That first offer helps establish a range of acceptable counteroffers, and any future offers will use that initial number as an anchor or focal point.

According to one study, making an excessively high wage request at the beginning really led to greater salary offers in the end.

It Has a Bigger Impact than Just Money

Beyond our money and shopping choices, the anchoring effect affects many aspects of our daily life. For example:

- *How old should your children be before you allow them to date, for instance? Your child claims that their peers are dating at 14, but you were brought up to think that 16 was the minimum age for dating. The anchoring effect makes you think that 16 is the earliest age at which a young person should be permitted to date.*

- *How long do you think you'll be alive? You could assume that you will live a long life if both of your parents lived to be very old. This anchoring point may induce you to overlook the fact that, compared to you, your parents led healthier, more active lifestyles that undoubtedly contributed to their lifespan.*

How much TV time should your kids get every day? If you grew up watching a lot of television, it could seem more normal for your children to spend hours a day riveted to the screen.

What condition is causing a patient's prolonged pain? The anchoring effect can affect how well a doctor diagnoses a patient's condition since their initial assessments of the patient's symptoms can establish an anchor point that influences all subsequent evaluations.

The anchoring effect has a significant influence on all of our decisions, from those regarding the products we purchase to those regarding our daily preferences for how to live our lives.

Consider the potential impact of the anchoring bias on your decisions the next time you are trying to make a significant decision. Are you choosing based on an existing anchor point, or are you giving all the information available and all the possibilities enough thought?

CHAPTER 5

What is cognitive bias?

When people absorb and interpret information from their environment, they can make systematic errors in cognition that have an impact on their decisions and judgements. This phenomenon is known as cognitive bias.

Although powerful, the human brain has its limits. Your brain tries to make information processing as simple as possible, which frequently results in cognitive biases. Biases frequently serve as generalizations that facilitate quick decision-making and aid in making sense of the world.

- **A few of these biases have to do with memory.** For a variety of reasons, the way you recall an experience may be skewed, which can then result in biased thinking and decision-making.

- **Other cognitive biases may be connected to attention issues**. People must be choosy about what they pay attention to in the world around them since attention is a finite resource.

Because of this, unnoticeable biases may infiltrate your thinking and affect how you perceive the world.

Amos Tversky and Daniel Kahneman, two psychologists, initially introduced the idea of cognitive bias in 1972. Since then, researchers have identified numerous forms of biases that influence judgment in a variety of contexts, such as social behaviour, cognition, behavioural economics, education, management, healthcare, business, and finance.

Logic Fallacy vs. Cognitive Bias

Logic fallacies and cognitive biases are two different concepts that are occasionally confused. A logical fallacy results from a flaw in an argument's logic, whereas cognitive biases are the result of thought processing flaws that are frequently caused by memory, attention, attribution, and other mental errors.

Signs

Cognitive bias is present in everybody. Although it may be simpler to identify in others, it is crucial to understand that it can have an impact on your thinking as well. The following are some indications that you might be subject to cognitive bias:

- Only reading news articles that support your viewpoints
- Accusing others as the cause of your problems
- Giving others credit for their success while claiming personal credit for your own achievements.
- Assuming that everyone else holds the same views or values as you do

Acknowledging that you know everything there is to know about a subject after learning only a bit about it. You want to believe that you are unbiased, logical, and able to take in and evaluate all the information that is available to you while you are making judgements and decisions about the world around you. Unfortunately, sometimes these biases cause us to make terrible decisions and judgements.

Types

Find out more about a few of the cognitive biases that affect people the most frequently.

• **Actor-observer bias:** This is the propensity to explain your own acts in terms of external reasons while explaining the motivations behind other people's actions. For instance, you might think that others' high cholesterol levels are caused by bad nutrition and inactivity while you ascribe your own to genetics.

• **Anchoring bias:** This is the propensity to place an excessive amount of weight on the first bit of knowledge you are exposed to. For instance, if you discover the typical cost of a car is a certain amount; you might stop looking for better offers because you will consider any sum below that to be a fantastic deal. By presenting the initial piece of information for consideration, you can leverage this bias to influence the expectations of others.

• **Attention bias:** This is the propensity to focus on certain items while neglecting others. For instance, while choosing a car, you might focus on how the outside and inside look and feel, but disregard the vehicle's safety record and fuel efficiency.

• The availability heuristic gives information that comes to mind rapidly more weight. You tend to overestimate the possibility and likelihood of similar situations happening in the future and give this information more weight.

• **Confirmation bias**: This is the tendency to favour information that supports your current opinions while rejecting evidence that contradicts them.

• The false consensus effect is the propensity to exaggerate the degree to which others concur with you.

• **Functional fixedness:** This is the propensity to think of things as only functioning in one way. For instance, you might not think to use a large wrench to push a nail into the wall if you don't have a hammer. If you don't have a corkboard to pin things to, you could assume you don't need thumbtacks and fail to explore their various use. This might also apply to how people perform their jobs, such as failing to see that a personal assistant has the aptitude to take on a leadership position.

• **Halo effect:** How you perceive someone as a whole affects how you feel and consider their character. This is particularly true when a person's physical appeal affects how you perceive their other traits.

• **Misinformation effect:** This is the propensity for information learned after an event to obstruct recall of the original event. It is simple for what you learn about the incident from others to sway your recall. A scepticism in eyewitness accounts has developed as a result of knowledge of this phenomenon.

• **Optimism bias:** This prejudice makes you think that you are more likely to succeed than your peers and that you are less likely to experience bad luck.

• **Self-serving bias:** This is the propensity to place the blame for negative outcomes on outside factors and to take credit for positive outcomes. For instance, when you win a poker hand, it's because of your ability to gauge the other players' intentions and understand the odds, and when you lose, it's because you were dealt a bad hand.

• **The Dunning-Kruger effect:** This describes persons who overestimate their intelligence and abilities. For instance, when they fail to acknowledge their own skill. Multiple biases may occasionally have an impact on your judgment and thought processes. For instance, you can incorrectly recall an incident (the disinformation effect) and believe that everyone else remembers it the same way (the false consensus effect).

Causes

Making even the most straightforward decision would take a lot of time if you had to consider every alternative. Because of the sheer volume of information in the environment and the complexity of the world around you, it is occasionally important to rely on some mental shortcuts that enable you to act swiftly.

Although there are many various factors that can contribute to cognitive biases, heuristics such as these frequently play a significant influence. They can frequently be surprisingly correct, yet they can also cause cognitive mistakes.

Additional elements that may also fuel these biases include:

- Emotions
- Individual motivations
- Limits on the mind's ability to process information
- Social pressures

As people age, their cognitive flexibility may become less, which could lead to an increase in cognitive bias.

Impact of Cognitive Bias

Thinking that is skewed might result from cognitive biases. For instance, a variety of biases frequently impact beliefs in conspiracies. However, not all cognitive biases are harmful. Many of these biases, according to psychologists, have an adaptive function in that they facilitate speedy decision-making. If we are in a dangerous or threatening scenario, this may be essential.

For instance, if you are walking down a dark alley and a dark shadow appears to be following you, cognitive bias may cause you to believe that the shadow is a thief and that you should leave the area right away. In instances where judgments need to be made fast, using mental shortcuts can frequently help you avoid danger. The black shadow may have simply been generated by a flag fluttering in the air.

Guidelines for Combating Cognitive Bias

According to research, cognitive training can reduce cognitive biases in the mind. You can do a number of things to assist in overcoming biases that could affect your judgment and decision-making, such as:

• **Being conscious of bias:** Take into account how biases may affect your judgment. In one study, researchers gave participants advice and knowledge to help them comprehend these biases and how they affect judgments. According to the study's findings, this kind of training can successfully minimize cognitive bias's negative impacts by 29%.

• **Examining the variables that affect your choices:** Do they include something like arrogance or self-interest? Making better decisions may result from considering the factors that influenced your decisions.

• **Fighting your prejudices:** If you discover that certain things are influencing your decisions, concentrate on actively fighting your biases. What are some of the elements you missed? Do you place too much emphasis on some variables? Do you disregard pertinent information because it contradicts your opinion? You can become a more critical thinker by considering these issues and confronting your prejudices.

What is cognitive in psychology?

The Science of How We Think

The study of how individuals think is the focus of the field of cognitive psychology. This area of psychology investigates a wide range of mental functions, such as how humans reason, speak, pay attention to details, and perceive their surroundings.

This page describes cognitive psychology, its background, and the current research agenda. Additionally, it discusses some of the real-world uses for cognitive psychology research and possible careers in the subject.

Studying internal mental processes, such as those involved in perception, thought, memory, attention, language, problem-solving, and learning, is called cognitive psychology.

Researchers can better understand how the human brain functions by knowing how people think and absorb information. It also enables psychologists to create fresh strategies for assisting persons with psychological issues.

For instance, psychologists are able to come up with methods that make it simpler for persons with attention challenges to increase their focus and concentration by realizing that attention is both a selective and finite resource.

Cognitive Psychology Topics
Cognitive psychologists investigate a wide range of issues pertaining to thought processes. A few of these are:

- Speech perception
- Speech-based behaviour
- Decision-making
- Forgetting
- Information processing
- Language learning
- Memory
- Problem-solving
- Information processing

CHAPTER 6

How Can You Use a Bias in Communication?

How to easily arouse desire in others by utilizing a
hidden cognitive bias

If a bias leads to poor judgment, it is negative. Are you
attempting to convince a boardroom to accept your
proposal? Obviously, you don't consider a purchase to be
a poor decision. (Or perhaps you do; in that case, choose
a different field of business or at the very least promote a
better product.)

Would it be beneficial for them to listen to you? Then, it
is ethical to manipulate one (or all 25) of their biases
such that they turn on especially in your favour,
persuading them to pay attention to you.
In order to influence people's perceptions, you can use a
bias in communication by turning it on in their brains.
Need a good example? Let's talk about biases and how to
use them.

Bias #1: Tendency toward Reward and Punishment

It is what? We develop habits that help us, keep us safe, or do both.

What source does it have? Human life is about making decisions about actions and then reaping rewards or suffering from them.

We evolved to seek gains in all circumstances and avoid losses because of the inherent, unalienable, intrinsic essence of our existence in this universe. Loss is the more powerful motivator of the two. Why? Loss hurts more than a similar gain does for us, often even twice as much. Another instance of loss aversion.

How do you communicate with it? You will become a better communicator than the great majority of your professional rivals with just this tactic. That's correct, you distinguish yourself from the bulk of people who lack effective communication skills by grasping this one basic idea.

What is the plan? Inform individuals that following your instructions will be advantageous and will shield them from harm. Inform them that failing to do so will result in the loss of a reward. And keep in mind that your persuasive power increases in proportion to the amount of gain or loss at risk.

Bias #2: Favouritisms and Love Tendency

It is what? People we love or admire are more convincing, and we tend to overlook their flaws and shortcomings.

What source does it have? We are sociable animals that have grown up around other people. This psychological inclination developed because it provided an evolutionary benefit (which helps us survive and thus pass on our genes containing the tendency). What is the benefit? **Stronger** human connections defending us in times of need.

How do you communicate with it? being likable How? Isn't it a rather difficult request? Could you just turn on likeability? Is it similar to a light switch? Obviously not. However, the next plan of action is as simple as turning a switch.

The tactic? I refer to it as the "two **most**." Discuss openly with them their **favourite** and least **favourite** things. This brings back the earlier bias. Check out how these tactics work together for better persuasion.
Talk to them about obtaining their top preferences and avoiding their top dislikes. Simple, yes? But imagine if someone asked you about your two greatest strengths.

You wouldn't be able to help but be drawn to them, would you?

Bias #3: Hatred and Disliking Tendency

It is what? People we despise are less compelling to us because we tend to emphasize their flaws and downplay their virtues.

What source does it have? This is a speculative explanation that hasn't been verified by science. This is simply my hunch. Because it stimulates the like and loving tendency, which aids in our survival by fostering stronger human relationships, the dislike and hating tendency evolved.

The tendency to dislike and hate has no benefit by itself. However, it triggers something that does. How can we fall in love with someone we hate? This is how it works: You dislike person X, you learn that person Y also despises person X, and suddenly you two are great friends.

In other words, the predisposition to dislike and hate enhances the relationships among the people who share the same animosity, which can enable those who belong to the in-group survive. Why? Because they have greater relationships with other in-group members due to their propensity for liking and adoring them. Time and time again, historical catastrophes have resulted from this.

Who are the immediate winners? Participants in the in-group.

How do you communicate with it? People who dislike a source will automatically reject its beliefs. And, dare I say it, you can make use of this. I may just advise you to stay out of harm's way. But that is pointless and clear. I'll reveal this tactic instead: Inform them that a source they despise attacked your stance. It's a technique known as inoculation, which is the practice of encouraging people to vehemently defend a viewpoint by making a feeble attack.

A case study? Now, [insert hated individual] will inform you that my position is [insert criticism]. But…” How does this function? Because by telling people that you were attacked by someone they despise, you remove any potential resistance to your position. It's sly, isn't it?

Bias #4: Avoiding doubt tendencies

It is what? We tend to steer clear of uncertainty. We ignore contradictory information, lean toward clear-cut "truths," pick sources of "truth" at random, and jump to conclusions too soon to avoid uncertainty, where we become entrenched no matter what we hear.

What source does it have? Our propensity to preserve cognitive resources is the cause of this. Why did we develop the ability to save mental resources? We need our wits to be quick and alert in a life-threatening emergency, not sluggish from the pressure of inconsequential choices. In actuality, our propensity to preserve cognitive resources is the root of all prejudices.

Why? They are all abbreviations.

How do you communicate with it? People are drawn to communicators without a doubt. Can you see where this is going?

Consider this: Why do people with little else going for them but excessive confidence rise to leadership positions? Why do people treat the arrogant, brash, and articulate moron seriously merely because he exudes confidence, as if he weren't still a fool? Why do we believe a statement that seems confident but is rejected when we detect even the slightest hint of uncertainty in the speaker's voice? Because we steer clear of uncertainty.

Therefore, how do you make this bias in communication active? Simple but effective: Show assurance in your argument. Speak without holding back. Speak up loud, firmly, and with considerable self-assurance. Your words, voice, and body language should all reflect this.

People will come to you naturally. They won't have any control over it. They will gravitate toward you because of your confidence because they can sense your lack of uncertainty.

Bias #5: Inconsistency Avoidance Tendency

It is what? People tend to refrain from acting contrary to their previous behaviour.

What source does it have? Our intrinsic urge as humans to create artificially orderly worlds in which we always behaved correctly (thus there is no need to be inconsistent with our former selves) in order to reduce confusion and conserve cognitive resources. By telling ourselves, "I probably thought this action through the first time, therefore this time, I'll trust my past-self," we can also save mental resources.
How do you communicate with it? Use signs of consistency. What are markers of consistency? Statements connecting your planned action to the audience's past behaviour. Make it appear as though

accomplishing what you want would be consistent with their pattern of similar behaviour: "You've probably always [insert related action; consistency justification here]." The reality is that [insert your plan] is really just continuing this legacy of good deeds because...

Bias #6: Curiosity Tendency

It is what? Particularly if we are aware of something we don't know, we desire to know. For instance, you would be more interested if I mentioned, "There are __ tons of bananas on Earth," rather than if I said nothing at all.

What source does it have? Evolution, seen a pattern here yet? It's funny how pattern recognition evolved with us.

Why? Once again, to preserve mental energy. But how does it evolve? Knowing more, a result of a curious mind, aids in our survival and the continuation of our genetic heritage. So, the genes that cause curiosity continue to exist.

How do you communicate with it? Open-ended rhetorical inquiries An open-loop rhetorical inquiry is what? I've only used one. Want to speak to someone who has their whole attention? Want to dominate the room and command respect? Apply these. They are effective because they highlight a knowledge gap, which strengthens and attracts interest.

The reward and punishment tendency is also activated by the following particular formula: How may other [insert audience description] obtain [insert advantage] and avoid [insert loss]? How do other small business owners, for instance, increase their customer base by five times while preventing the collapse of their supply chains?

What is the most effective way to [insert goal] without encountering [insert particular challenge]?

"Why does [insert unexpected incident here] happen the way it does?"

What is the secret information about [insert topic] that the "experts" won't share with you?

Bias #7: Kantian Fairness Tendency

It is what? We have a propensity to think that everything should be fair, to treat people the way we want to be treated, and to become terribly, irrationally angry when someone doesn't act fairly.
What source does it have? Anything that encourages harmonious interactions among people is beneficial to our survival. Because humans survive and reproduce

when we have certain traits or tendencies, the genes encoding them are passed on.

How do you communicate with it? The activation of emotions draws the eye. And the strongest emotional force is typically produced by negative feelings. As a skilled communicator by this point, you can use this emotional power as a spur to action. Without an emotional motivation, people do not act.

You can't command respect, influence, convince, explain clearly, or compel people to take action if you can't arouse their emotions. Convince individuals that fairness has been broken against them if your Kantian Fairness Tendency creates extreme offense when fairness is violated, intense offense is a highly arousing feeling, and high emotional arousal is required for effective persuasion.

How? Using this straightforward, tried-and-true process: The Victim-Perpetrator-Benevolence Triad is what I refer to as.

Initially: Victim. Let people know why they were treated unfairly and why they are the victims of a breach in the law of justice. Don't mention that someone someplace treated someone else unfairly. Let them know they are helpless.

Secondly, the perpetrator. Who is to blame for this? Who victimized them directly, exactly? With a distinct, colourful perpetrator and a clear description of how they violated the law, this triad is stronger.

Third part: Benevolence. Present yourself (and, if you are selling something, your product) as a saviour for the victim who will punish the offender and bring justice back to the world. Describe how you can assist: Don't just say, "I can help," but be specific about how you can address both the victim's issue and the faulty judicial system (s). Watch how you can relatively easily activate the most complex psychological machinery, leading to vastly improved communication.

Bias #8: Envy and Jealousy Tendency

It is what? We detest seeing things or accomplishments that we desire for ourselves in someone else's hands.

What source does it have? Our attempts to meet our infinite desires with a constrained resource pool due to our innate urge to compete for scarce resources.
How do you communicate with it? You can quickly add still additional emotional pull to your offer, making it more attractive and captivating, by taking advantage of the predisposition toward jealously and jealousy.

How? By provoking someone's inclination for jealousy and envy, how can you make them want something intensely? How can you instantly improve the appeal of your offer so that you can charge more for the same thing? (You and your ideas are also products.)

This is how: Use the phrase "[insert competition] has [insert what you are offering] and they have safeguarded themselves from [insert harm] while benefiting from [insert benefit]" to describe your situation.

A case study? Let's take a cue from Mad Men, the highly regarded television program. (It's my preferred program. I've definitely watched all 7 seasons—each with about 15 hours of content—ten times by this point. If you want to, you can do the math.

Sterling Cooper Draper Pryce (SCDP), the protagonist's advertising firm, is engaged in a struggle for market share with Cutler Gleason and Chaough (CGC). Anyone attempting to sell CGC something could incite their inclination toward envy and jealousy by doing the following: In order to insulate them from the rat race of obscurity and to take advantage of a flood of new business with large billings and a national presence, SCDP recently hired a professional branding service.

Now, CGC wants the service not only for its intrinsic advantages but also because SCDP already has it and they do not. Cool, huh? Your ability to persuade others increases as you develop more convincing reasons for them to want your offer. Nobody even implied that you had to express your noble emotions. Jealousy is effective. However, there is also the "golden-rule" emotion, or the propensity for reciprocation. Now let's go on to it.

Bias #9: Reciprocation Tendency

It is what? Positive or negative activities are intended to be rewarded.

What source does it have? Evolution, it strengthens ties between people, much like the predisposition toward liking and loving. When those relationships are broken, it results in retribution in the form of unfavourable reciprocation, disincentivizing treachery.

How do you communicate with it? This is a simple one. And it has tremendous power. Great simplicity and enormous effectiveness condensed into one tactic: If ever I heard a good mixture, this is it.

How can you make others want to do favours for you until the reciprocation inclination kicks in? How can you ensure that your business communications are received with undivided attention, complete respect, and increased rates of compliance? How do you attract business chances to yourself and have prospects draw toward you?

It's easy: Do something for them. a complimentary snack. A price cut. A free white paper or market study. A no-cost consultation free recommendation
There are no free meals in life: These aren't actually all free. There is a cost: psychologically compelling need to return the favour in the future.

If you're conversing with them, your convincing arguments will receive a lot more sincere consideration, and they'll give you a lot more consideration and respect.

Bias #10: Influence from Mere Association

It is what? We assume a new item is also nice when it is grouped with other good things. We presume a new item is also terrible when it is grouped with other bad things. In essence: By extrapolating from its surroundings, we can determine a new item's characteristics.

What source does it have? We must protect our mental resources.

How do you communicate with it? Semantic sentiment mapping is a difficult, intricate, and highly skilled method. It uses extremely obscure vocabulary, balancing calculations, "localized sentiment scores," and mathematics.

Willing to learn it? If you've learned anything about yourself thus far, it should be this: Your brain tries to save mental energy rather than expend it on mastering semantic sentiment analysis. Or perhaps you currently have a strong desire to learn due to your curiosity.

I'll choose the middle road. I'll give you the basic minimum of the technique and explain how it dramatically increases your persuasiveness by activating influence by mere association.

You deal with two factors when influencing someone. the initial? An alternative to your suggestion, such as doing nothing. The next? your suggestion.

You want to keep them from running straight for the first while also nudging them in that direction. How? Put words that are offensive next to the alternative. Give examples of the unpleasant anecdotes. Put adjectives like "abysmal," "painful," "difficult," "tiresome," "self-defeating," and "unnecessary" in your writing.

They are consciously influenced by the central idea of your message—that the alternative is appalling. But they also detect compelling associations subliminally. And associations alone can have an impact. The connection?

The alternative is surrounded by a mass of unfavourable things, so it must also be unfavourable.

Reverse it: Include encouraging language and tales with your proposal. Influence gained through simple association disempowers any alternatives while empowering your proposal.

Bias #11: Simple, Pain-Avoiding Psychological Denial

It is what? Psychologically upsetting information is frequently ignored or denied until it is tolerable.
What source does it have? We have an innate urge to keep our minds sharp and flexible, free from consuming worries.
How do you communicate with it? In order to persuade, you must urge a solution to a dilemma. The secret of persuasive success is as follows: The solution is more appealing the more damaging the problem is. Unless one thing stops you: Their tendency to deny the issue completely prevents them from seeing it.

You have a significant challenge here. Huge. Why? You can't generate the emotional pull required for motivation and, eventually, action until you overcome the propensity toward denial and validate the issue.

How can you get over your predisposition to deny? How do you ensure that your persuading arguments don't fail to deliver? How can you safeguard yourself from the main deterrent to persuasion?

Combining two approaches into one Prospect-driven hypothetical admissions supported by unshakeable evidence Ask yourself questions such, "How would you be affected if [insert problem] were true?" and "Would you recognize that [insert problem] is indeed a severe threat if [insert proof] were the case?" These are fictitious admissions motivated by prospects.

Then, use statements like, "Well, I agree with you. Sadly, this is the situation. In accordance with [insert source], [insert proof] is accurate. But [insert more evidence] and [insert more evidence] are also relevant. Unfortunately, [insert problem] is extremely real and very detrimental, and as a result, [insert their exact words from when they answered the first question speculating on the impact] impacts you. "How come this works? It asks them to imagine potential negative consequences of a situation that might arise; something that might be accurate but is probably not. Until you can demonstrate that it is genuine. By imagining the issue in an idealized setting, you can get through psychological denial. In a fictitious world, psychological denial is not possible. The reason why?

Bias #12: Excessive Self-Regard Tendency

It is what? We all believe we are better than average. What source does it have? It is self-fulfilling to be confident. Self-belief helped you survive 2,000 years ago if you overconfidently thought you could survive a mammoth hunt. Consequently, you dispersed the genes.

Similar to animals, humans have an inherent propensity to fight (both physically and verbally) but only when they believe their adversary won't respond.

Overconfidence in ourselves tends to make us combative. So we avoid conflict in the first place, live, and pass on a propensity for exaggerated self-importance.

How do you communicate with it? People enjoy seeing symmetry in worldviews. Declare it. You'll be more persuasive in their eyes. Do you still have the tendency to like and love? This makes it active.

How can you explain symmetry in worldviews? How can you convince them that you share their worldview? It's easy: Match their predisposition to view themselves too highly. How? Not by exaggerating your own importance, but by exaggerating theirs.

Describe your company as "ahead of the curve," "cutting-edge," or "innovative." Indicate that their staff members are "ambitious," "competent," and "above average." Describe your institution as "high-end," "prestigious," and "impactful."

Bias #13: Over-Optimism Tendency

It is what? Excessive optimism is a characteristic of all people.

What source does it have? It enables us to save our mental energy. It is linked to numerous mental heuristics and cognitive biases. It lessens the stress of surviving on a hostile planet.

How do you communicate with it? Those with vision are followed. If you don't sell your vision, you can't persuade. In order for them to fully appreciate the untapped potential that your suggestion can help them realize, you must "screen-share" your mental movie with them. Also keep in mind that the vision must be related to reaching their objectives.

How does overconfidence relate to this? By engaging this prejudice, how can you come across as a compelling communicator and a perceptive visionary? How can you use it to exert great influence and win over anyone easily?

It's easy: Don't be shy in outlining your vision. Be out front about the abundance of advantages. Use the authority this provided you to jump into vision-sharing, upbeat and overwhelmingly positive vision-sharing, after providing some flimsy proof; some quantitative evidence from reputable sources. They can expect your positivity. People are excited about this.

Bias #14: Deprival Super reaction Tendency

It is what? Loss-aversion. Gains and new pay-outs are something we would rather avoid. Occasionally twice as much. A $1,000 loss might be twice as unpleasant as a $1,000 gain. And when we lose something, we react with an uncontrollable, irrational passion in an effort to make up for it. We also frequently exert excessive amounts of effort in an attempt to reach a target that we narrowly missed.

What source does it have? Two thousand years ago, activities related to guarding what we had—territories, resources, food, members of our tribe—probably contributed more to our survival than actions aimed at acquiring more. We are therefore genetically and evolutionarily programmed to minimize risk and play the game of life cautiously.

How do you communicate with it? Increase the risks and describe what they stand to lose. However, we already spoke about this. What is an alternative? The tactic of "You narrowly missed it!" Remind them of how close they came to reaching a goal. They were inches from achieving a deeply wanted objective, yet they just missed it. Present your plan as putting the "nearly there!" objective within their grasp for good.
Having said that, this next tactic is among the most effective persuasion techniques I've ever learned. It is empirically supported and shown to routinely persuade people to act in predictable ways, much like all of these cognitive biases.

Bias #15: Social-Proof Tendency

It is what? We look to others for guidance as we follow the crowd.

What source does it have? This inclination has two important evolutionary demands genetically encoded for it. We must conserve our mental energy, and a tribe must provide security. Because we defer to the opinions of the masses rather than utilizing our own judgment, social proof conserves mental energy. Second, it helps us maintain our "group-member status" because it allows us to blend in with the crowd when we act in accordance with the crowd.

How do you communicate with it? Make remarks that show people doing or thinking in the way you want your prospects to act or think.

87 % of [insert audience identifier, such as 'small company owners'] say that [insert the problem you solve] is a significant drain on resources.

"On Amazon, 97 % of our clients gave us five stars." "30,000 satisfied customers have used our product so far,"

Statistics serve as quantifiable social proof. What is high-quality social proof? What a select few particular people in detail said quantitatively, there are more good reviews; qualitatively, what one of the reviews specifically states. Which one ought to you choose? Erroneous dilemma Apply both.

Bias #16: Contrast-Miscreation Tendency

It is what? We don't evaluate things based on their inherent merits, but rather on how they stack up against benchmarks.
What source does it have? This is a by-product of the way our brains work. It may result in frequent and foolish errors of judgment. Without a point of comparison, we cannot appraise anything on its own.

Before learning that our co-worker earns $62,000, we are content with our $60,000 pay. But regardless of what anyone else earns, $60,000 remains $60,000, no matter what. Sadly, our judgment doesn't operate in that way. To draw conclusions, we constantly make use of comparisons.

How do you communicate with it? This bias permeates all forms of communication. There are countless ways to trigger it. But which is the most convincing? How can you make the contrast-miscreation propensity work in your favour to elicit fervent and enthusiastic action?

How can you persuade others to view things your way, act the way you desire, and support your professional advancement? This tremendously potent psychological heuristic is activated by the path-contrast structure in a very persuasive manner.

What exactly are you doing when you persuade someone? Attempting to influence someone to choose one course over another. And path one alone has no purpose and cannot persuade. The true persuasion occurs when path one is compared to path two.

The easy, uncomplicated, sequential route contrast procedure? Determine path one or what you want them to do, as the first step. Describe it. The second step is to choose the alternate path. Describe it. Step three is to describe the advantages of path one. Step four is to describe the drawbacks of method 2. Step five: Repeat steps three and four as necessary to increase contrast. It's a straightforward mould with step-by-step instructions that immediately engages a highly persuasive and significant cognitive function.

Bias #17: Stress-Misinfluence Tendency

It is what? Under pressure, we make rash, irrational, and extreme decisions.

What source does it have? When a sober-toothed tiger charged in front of us 2,000 years ago, putting us under a lot of cognitive stress, we had to act quickly. Struggle or flee? (Probably flee: Its name contains the word "sober-tooth"...)

The amygdala, a region of the brain, activates under this circumstance. The prefrontal brain, which conducts careful, systematic, and sluggish logical computations, is turned off.

The issue? Even when reasoning is required to address the cause of the stress, such as during a sales pitch or interview, the amygdala activates and inhibits reason; it is not a sober-toothed tiger (agility-demanding).

How do you communicate with it? After causing stress, relieve it. Set the bar higher before providing a way out. Draw a graphic picture of the issue, and then offer a fix. Put pressure on it, and then let it go.

"You have a difficulty. This is a very bad thing for the following reasons: [Stress-induce]. Yet I can assist you.

Here's how I can stop these negative effects: [Stress-ease]. "

They are in a mental state of rapid response when stressed, which makes it simpler to persuade someone through emotion and induce an "impulse buy." When faced with stress, people will impulsively turn to your answer if and only if they have anything to run away from. If they don't receive any stressful information that makes them feel like they need to flee, they won't take the risk.

Bias #18: Availability MisWeighing Tendency

It is what? We prioritize the evidence that immediately comes to mind.

What source does it have? Preservation of mental capacity. It's a mental shortcut that, in most situations, results in a rough, approximate, "good enough" judgment. Other instances? It causes grave errors in judgment.
How do you communicate with it? A quick recap of the 13 tactics I discussed in the chapter on availability is provided below:

"Strategy #1: Tell Stories
Strategy #2: Use Pathos
Strategy #3: Use Sententia
Strategy #4: Project Images
Strategy #5: Make it Personal

Strategy #6: Keep it Simple
Strategy #7: Provide Tangible Takeaways
Strategy #8: Always Summarize
Strategy #9 Invoke Fear
Strategy #10: Invoke Desire
Strategy #11: Use Mnemonics
Strategy #12: Make it Eloquent
Strategy #13: Visualize Data"

Bias #19: Use It or Lose It Tendency

It is what? If we don't use the information we've stored, we lose it.

What source does it have? We gradually discard the knowledge we don't need in order to preserve our limited supply of brain resources.

How do you communicate with it? This is a general piece of advice, not something you use in dialogue. Read more about these tactics. However, if you don't use the insights, you eventually lose them.

What does it mean in terms of communication? Make your point in a useful way. Make it instructive. Give folks knowledge they can utilize to enhance their life. They will remember it. Instead of losing it, they'll use it.

Bias #20: Drug Misinfluence Tendency

It is what? Drug use impairs thinking.
What source does it have? Drugs.

How do you communicate with it? I'm required by law to warn you from drugging your audience. In all honesty, there isn't much you can do to ethically trigger this propensity. It was only on Munger's 25 that I felt the need to include it.

Coffee is a good idea. When appropriate, perhaps some alcoholic beverages to ease a conversation. Your audience may become more attentive and experience a dopamine rush if you serve them coffee. People are more receptive to persuasive arguments the happier they are. Reciprocity, likeability, and other relevant biases are also activated. We'll probably stick with this piece of advice: The only ethical way to activate this one is to offer coffee when you have the ability to do so.

Bias #21: Senescence-Misinfluence Tendency

It is what? Older adults are more likely than younger persons to have flawed cognition.

What source does it have? Older age.

How do you communicate with it? I'm not even going to try on this one. He includes it in his list of 25, so I did. It cannot be used in communication. The remaining four biases, which are directly pertinent to persuasive communication, are among the 25's most convincing.

Bias #22: Authority-Misinfluence Tendency

It is what? We are persuaded by authority figures. What source does it have? This presumably made it easier for tribes and groups to form more productive and organized relationships, which helped us survive.

Additionally, it preserves mental energy. To understand every aspect of medicine when we are ill would tax our cognitive abilities. Employing a specialist for outsourcing is more effective.
How do you communicate with it? This one has a ton of power. If someone in a position of authority commands them to, most people will comply. It is a component of the horror of war.

We pay attention to doctors, coaches, and specialists because they are qualified to do so. We believe what a physician or scientist claims to be true.

How can you make use of this well-documented psychological inclination for stronger communication?

How can you utilize it to persuade people quickly? How do you convey your authority without boasting and win people over right away?

What are your credentials, exactly? What is your background? Why ought people to believe you? Respond to these inquiries. Additionally, there is a concept known as authority-transfer: You take on some of the authority of the arguments you make, the sources of your expertise, and the group you speak for. Keep it in mind and combine the presentation of direct authority with the activation of authority-transfer.

Now, why do we put things off? How do you get others to comply with your wishes "later"? Let's look into bias 23 to find the solution.

Bias #23: Twaddle Tendency

It is what? Spending a lot of time on pointless tasks Procrastinating.

What source does it have? Our fundamental desire to minimize cognitive load. Why put it off? Because it's easy on the mind. Our discipline is tested when we begin the following task or conduct. Our field operates like a limited budget: It ultimately runs dry. It's simply easier to twaddle after a hard day when we know the next task will be mentally taxing.

How do you communicate with it? If you let this one continue, it will seriously hinder your ability to reach your objectives. It might make everything you say invalid. It can ruin an otherwise flawless pitch or presentation. Whatever else you say or do, it can undermine your attempts to persuade. The twaddle tendency has the power to scuttle everything, even if you engage the other biases, offer proof, logic, and emotional appeals, and even if they like you personally.
How can you prevent this? By addressing the "why now?" issue. What is the issue that so many communicators are having? They concentrate on the incorrect issue. They concentrate on providing an explanation for why. But that is untrue. Even if you can persuade someone to do something, they won't take action unless you can explain why now.

You can't make me want to explore the world by making excuses for me. Why? given that I already do. I don't want to tour the world right now, though. I must complete other tasks first (like earn the money I need to travel the world). Why should I do it now is the query I need to hear you address. Keep repeating to yourself, "'Why now?' not 'why?'" and you'll be OK.

Bias #24: Reason Respecting Tendency

It is what? Requests are respected, and we accept claims that are supported by logic.

What source does it have? Substitution is a technique humans employ to conserve cognitive resources. We replace a difficult question with one that is simple. How does this relate to the propensity that respects reason?

We replace it with the simple inquiry "is there a reason behind this?" regarding the challenging inquiry, "Is this a good and valid reason?" Even an erroneous rationale is frequently enough to convince someone.

How do you communicate with it? Offer justifications and meta-justifications. A meta-justifier is defined. Meta-justifications are amazingly persuasive, engrossing, and attention-grabbing. They defend the communication itself by saying: "I'm phoning today to let you know about..."

What does a common justifier do? The standard justifications are "[insert statement] because [insert explanation]," or "could you [insert request] because [insert reason]," respectively.

The single most crucial idea in this book is now in focus: Munger refers to this as the "Lollapalooza tendency."

Bias #25: The Lollapalooza Tendency

It is what? Any psychological tendency that encourages a specific activity is persuasive. When more people engage in the same behaviour, their persuasive power multiplies exponentially. It has a "lollapalooza impact," according to Munger. It occurs when several cognitive biases move in the same direction simultaneously.

What source does it have? It results from each bias's unique influence. Their persuasive power is greater than the sum of their parts. One plus one equals three applies in this situation.

How do you communicate with it? The other 24 cognitive biases can be activated by you. What then triggers the lollapalooza tendency? Engage all of the opposing biases at once and in the same direction. It's simple; you already know how to activate each one separately, and when you combine their persuasive power, the results will astound you. Additionally, not all 24 can be used. This is activated by even two at once.

How to speak eloquently and fluidly in any situation
Sometimes it may appear as though eloquence is
something you either have from birth or you don't. In
actuality, improving one's ability to communicate
eloquently takes time and work. The best part is that
anyone can learn it and get better at it.

Have you ever experienced being mesmerized by a
remarkable speaker's music of speech, poetry of words,
and resonance of voice? Then they most likely possess
the rare quality of eloquence.

We all want to be able to explain one clearly, whether
we're addressing a small group of co-workers or a large
audience, because it's in that specific zone of eloquence
when communication magic may occur.

What does it mean to communicate effectively?

A speaker with eloquence is one who is adept at using
language. They are aware of its complexities and
nuances and are able to use it to effectively and
persuasively convey their message.

A fantastic piece of music is analogous to listening to an
eloquent speaker. We often recall the message they
conveyed and the way they made us feel, and it might
make us happy.

It involves more than just speaking clearly and coherently. It is defined as "the quality of delivering a clear, forceful message" by the Cambridge Dictionary. Not only is the message being conveyed, but also its significance.

The finest thing is that everyone can improve their speaking ability. Although it's true that some people just have it easier and are strong public speakers naturally, anyone can develop this skill. It all depends on how much time and effort you put into it.

Why you should try to improve your eloquence

Being able to communicate in a way that people will pay attention can make a huge difference in both your personal and professional life. Eloquence is the ability to convey a message in such a way that it is taken seriously.

Eloquence can become a precious ability in the business. It can be the obstacle preventing you from receiving a raise. Or the means by which your team will hear your thoughts. You'll sound more confident overall, get your point of view heard, and become a better public speaker.

Tips to Speak More Eloquently

So, now that you are aware of the benefits of trying to better yourself and become an articulate speaker, the actual question arises. How can you speak more clearly?

Sadly, it appears to be one of those traits that you either have or don't. However, as has already been stated, this is not always the case. It probably won't come to you as naturally if you have trouble speaking in front of groups of people. But it takes practice, just like most things in life.

Perseverance and public speaking will be necessary. You must persist even if you don't notice much improvement the first time. You will only truly master the talent if you are constantly forced to encounter challenges.

You may improve your eloquence by using these 9 simple methods. Although there is no easy path, you can attempt implementing each of these punctual strategies one at a time. Just keep in mind that the following time will be simpler the more you practice.

Sometimes it may appear as though eloquence is something you either have from birth or you don't. In actuality, improving one's ability to communicate eloquently takes time and work. The best part is that anyone can learn it and get better at it. Here are simple suggestions to help you speak more persuasively and deliver a message that people will truly want to hear.

What really is "speaking eloquently"?

It involves more than just speaking clearly and coherently. It is defined as "the quality of delivering a clear, forceful message" by the Cambridge Dictionary. Not only is the message being conveyed, but also its significance.

The finest thing is that everyone can improve their speaking ability. Although it's true that some people just have it easier and are strong public speakers naturally, anyone can develop this skill. It all depends on how much time and effort you put into it.

Why you should try to improve your eloquence

Being able to communicate in a way that people will pay attention can make a huge difference in both your personal and professional life. Eloquence is the ability to convey a message in such a way that it is taken seriously.

Eloquence can become a precious ability in the business. It can be the obstacle preventing you from receiving a raise. Or the means by which your team will hear your thoughts. You'll sound more confident overall, get your point of view heard, and become a better public speaker.

1- Less is better.

In this instance, the adage "less is more" is certainly applicable. It's simple to succumb to the need to sound smarter by using extremely flowery and grandiloquent language. Most likely, this isn't even a conscious action. Just attempting to demonstrate our knowledge of the subject at hand. It frequently indicates anxiety or self-doubt.

Consider it this way: Those who truly comprehend a difficult subject are not those who can quote a textbook word for word, but rather those who can explain a difficult subject in their own terms. What will really make a difference is your ability to analyse the knowledge and pass it down to your audience in a clear, simple manner. Your eloquence and the strength of your arguments will increase as your audience's comprehension increases.

When learning how to communicate more eloquently, using concise and clear vocabulary is essential for one very obvious reason. It lessens your likelihood of becoming caught up in oneself. The likelihood that you may eventually lose your train of thought increases with the complexity and length of the language. Simple doesn't always imply informal, and vice versa. Simply maintain a straightforward tone and you'll notice that you seem more confident and that your talks sound better and more dynamic as opposed to tripping over some unfamiliar terms.

Also, be careful to only use language you are truly familiar with. All of us have probably encountered the situation when we learn a new word but aren't entirely sure of what it means but it seems to fit the context of what we're trying to express. Even if the word sounds fine on its own, utilizing it improperly will make you appear unprofessional. Make sure you know how to pronounce a new word before using it. It's possible to understand a word's meaning simply by reading it, but if you've never heard it before, speaking it in public can be challenging.

2- Speak with clarity

Any form of communication is meant to be understood by the recipient(s) so that they can respond appropriately. Additionally, as mentioned in the preceding paragraph, being understood involves more than just making sure the other person understands the words you're using. It's also important to be able to physically comprehend the sounds you're producing and give them meaning. Your audience's ability to comprehend you will undoubtedly suffer if you stutter, speak too quietly, or murmur. Not only could that, but doing so make you appear unconfident and weaken your arguments. It's not uncommon for folks to make a few careless pronunciation errors when they're anxious or pressed for time. Make sure each syllable in a word is clearly pronounced. You'll come across as more attentive and professional just by doing this.

You might initially need to exert effort and it could appear challenging. But forcing yourself to focus on clearly pronouncing each and every syllable can gradually develop into a positive habit that can even improve your focus. And eventually, it'll feel rather natural to you. By practicing with tongue twisters, for instance, you can get better at this. It will eventually get easier when you are performing in front of an audience, the tougher they are when you are practicing.

3- Bring your words to life.

Being able to relate to your audience and express powerful feelings is a necessary component of being eloquent. Giving them something they can relate to is the quickest, most straightforward method to accomplish this. Making your speech feel alive can be accomplished in large part by using metaphors, similes, and references.

They don't have to be particularly intricate metaphors or allusions. In the end, what you're attempting to do is use a comparison to highlight a point you're attempting to make.

This might be challenging because it requires understanding your audience. The audience should be able to quickly understand your allusions without having to do an in-depth analysis that would take them away from what you are actually saying. References are available from every single source. Historical events, classical literature, and popular culture they can even add a little humour or make your presentation more entertaining. The only thing you should actually think about is whether or not your audience will be able to grasp them.

4- Leave the filler words out!

One of the worst errors a public speaker can make is using filler words. Words that don't really add any sense to what you're attempting to communicate are known as filler words. Like, you know, or "I mean," for instance.

When you're unsure of how to proceed, saying these kinds of things is more of a reflex action to break up an awkward pause. Additionally, filler words could simply be sounds. When unsure, it's normal to pause and add a "umm" to try to remember what comes next.

Despite how frequent they are, they are typically a very dangerous sign of uncertainty and unpreparedness. The worst part is that, after you've grown accustomed to them, it may be difficult to get rid of them. Filler words are one of the most prevalent barriers to speaking more eloquently among all potential obstacles.

The worst part is that once you start, you can't stop. You'll probably feel more anxious or frustrated if you become aware that you're utilizing filler words when speaking in front of an audience. This will most likely result in even more hesitancy and the use of filler words.

The second suggestion on this list, "consider before you speak," is the strongest defence against filler words.

5- Pre-meditated speech

You'd be shocked at how few people actually heed this advice, despite the fact that it may seem obvious. If you are aware that public speaking is not your strong suit, you must make advance plans if you know you will need to do so.

But it's also important to keep in mind that you might not have enough time to thoroughly arrange your presentation in advance. However, you ought to be able to identify your primary talking points at the very least.

It's less likely that you will find yourself hesitating in the middle of a speech if you can organize your train of thought. The simpler solution to stop using filler words forever is to plan out what you're going to say.

Sometimes you just need a couple of extra seconds. It's simple to become overwhelmed by an interruption or a question for which you are unprepared and to try to leave the situation as soon as possible. However, pausing before responding might actually do wonders for your appearance of being articulate and eloquent. You may, for instance, respond to a question with another inquiry.

The audience will be able to think about it and come up with their own solutions. However, it will also give you some time to gather your own ideas so you can respond more effectively and without hesitating or using extraneous filler words.

6- Speak slowly.

Another crucial aspect to consider while considering how to talk more eloquently is pacing. Rushing a little when we're anxious about something is entirely acceptable. However, speaking at a rapid pace frequently comes out as unprepared and uneasy. It could sound challenging, but self-control is the key.

Knowing how to use your voice and pace go hand in hand. Nothing is more monotonous than a presentation.

You must be able to effectively utilize all the incredible tools voice affords in order to be considered truly eloquent. Accentuation can be achieved through intonation. Voice volume, silences, and pauses there are numerous things you may do that will enhance your presentations.

In his TEDTalk on "The 110 strategies of communication and public speaking," David Phillips does a great job of communicating this. There is no better illustration of how the voice's numerous nuances and tones can significantly alter how a speech is delivered.

7- Feel assured and at ease

Even though scripting your entire presentation may make you feel more prepared (see tip #5), it might not be the best move. While it's important to consider your message in advance, having the entire presentation scripted is rarely the best course of action. There is a good chance that it will sound artificial or robotic.

Eloquence is about delivering a powerful message, and if it's excessively planned, you could be inclined to just recite it verbatim rather than putting real passion into it.

Furthermore, interruptions to speeches and presentations are inevitable. It's impossible to plan for every possible scenario, whether it's a question from someone or just that the conversation naturally veered off topic. Despite your best efforts, it is impossible to anticipate every possible inquiry. In these circumstances, relying excessively on a script may become more of a burden than a help. If you put too much effort into following a script and then realize that you can't, you'll probably feel disoriented and uncertain rather fast.

You must allow yourself some leeway for creativity. It could be challenging at first, but confidence is key. This may seem practically impossible if you lack confidence in your capacity for public speaking, but confidence is something that develops naturally as a result of satisfying experiences. You'll do better and gain more confidence the more you attempt. Focusing on the material is a helpful strategy for overcoming this self-doubt. You should feel secure in your understanding of the subject you're talking about, even if you don't have everything scripted and you don't feel sure in your presentation skills.

8- Observe your body language.

When it comes to confidence, body language can be really important. Even if you don't feel particularly confident, being aware of and in control of your body language might give the impression that you are. For instance, a public speaker's posture can significantly alter how they are regarded.

Additionally, you can stress particular details of what you're saying with your body language. An affirmation can easily be strengthened by using hand movements, for instance. To become more eloquent, you must physically reinforce what you're speaking aloud. When you speak in front of a crowd, people are watching you as well as hearing you. Additionally, a significant portion of the message you provide to them is through your body language.

On the other hand, there are certain other body language cues that can make you appear less articulate. One of the simplest ways to convey that you are not at all at ease is to fidget or appear restless in front of the audience. You will appear more eloquent the more you control the environment and your body language.

9- The most crucial piece of advice for improving one's oratory

After all is said and done, there is one thing that will significantly impact how well you talk in public and with eloquence. And more practice is exactly what this is.

When speaking in front of a crowd, confidence is crucial. And the only way to make it better is by having successful experiences. Even if it seems like you're not progressing as quickly or as much as you'd like, the more you practice, the more confidence you'll develop for upcoming presentations. When attempting to improve your talents, it might make a difference even if you simply believe that things went "a bit less badly" than they did the last time.
Record or, much better, film yourself speaking if you have the opportunity. Even though it could be uncomfortable at first, viewing yourself allows you to see yourself how your audience does. It's the simplest technique to identify your weaknesses and flaws. When you view something from the outside, you can notice things that you otherwise might not have observed.

How to look authoritative, trustworthy, and capable in 10 seconds by generating the halo effect

We tend to impute psychological traits to people based merely on how gorgeous they are, a phenomenon known as the "Halo Effect." In other words, the attractive man will be regarded as friendlier or smarter.

It's a phenomenon that happens without your awareness and can have a big impact on society, including your choice of mate, education, marketing, and even legal procedures.

The Halo Effect is what? You may see the Halo Effect as a mental shortcut that some areas of your brain use while making judgments about people. Based on one quality or attribute, you can assess and judge a person or thing, and you can extrapolate the remainder of their personal attributes from that one quality. This frequently has nothing to do with the true qualities of the person or product.

Knowing and comprehending this psychological phenomenon would enable us as humans to make decisions with greater objectivity and avoid cognitive biases.

Thorndike introduced the Halo Effect in the 1920s. After running several tests with the Army, Thorndike came up with this word.

The phenomena occur because the brain attempts to conserve energy by streamlining perceptual processes, not because we are foolish or credulous. This shortcut can be advantageous in some circumstances while, as with the Halo Effect, impairing our judgment in many others.

Illustrations of the Halo Effect

The first impressions or expectations we have of other individuals could be severely impacted by the Halo Effect.

When Susan Boyle, a singer, appeared on **Britain's Got Talent**, it was a recent instance of the Halo Effect.
If you've already watched the video, consider your initial reaction to her.

If you haven't already, Test your ability to withstand the Halo Effect.

When Susan entered the stage, nobody in the audience immediately noticed her. She didn't seem like the normal attractive, personable, and self-assured vocalist, but everyone was astounded when she opened her mouth to sing.

From the minute Susan entered the stage, both the judges and the audience knew what they thought of her. Nobody expected her to be talented, but after her performance, she left thousands of people speechless. This, in Martinez de Toda's opinion, is the best illustration of the Hale Effect and how it affects us as people.
When Susan Boyle initially entered the stage, what were your first thoughts? Did you manage to avoid making any judgments about her appearance or were you able to look past it?

Marketing and the Halo Effect

The Halo Effect can also be applied to "essential" objects, not just people. This is why so many companies look for celebrities to use or wear their products in advertisements. Have you ever questioned why Eva Longoria is in advertisements for cosmetics or why George Clooney is promoting a coffee maker? The marketing, public relations, and psychology teams within the corporation are aware of how to use the Halo Effect to their advantage.

Marketing firms that know that many people will go buy the coffee maker that George Clooney is advertising choose him or her because they find them to be appealing, charismatic, and nice.

Job interviews and the Halo Effect

In job interviews, The Halo Effect is extremely important. You've certainly heard the standard horror story of someone who was turned down for a job because they arrived at the interview with a coffee-stained blouse after spilling coffee on themselves on the way there. The opposite also occurs. If that student from your class barely made it through school, how did he land the job? Many persons with typically good looks have been hired for positions for which they may not have been qualified.

You'll learn below how to use the Halo Effect to your advantage during a job interview.

Reverse Halo Effect or the Devil Effect

The Devil Effect: What is it? Darkness exists without light. The Devil Effect, in contrast to the Halo Effect, which imparts a pleasant emotion or judgment, occurs when a person or thing is viewed negatively and bad features or characteristics are inferred because of a single quality or characteristic.

Politics are also significantly impacted by The Devil Effect. It's more difficult to appreciate the advantages or admirable deeds of a particular politician once you've established a bad view about them.

Advice on how to avoid being fooled by the "Halo Effect"

1. Be aware of your judgment.

Being aware of when you're incorrectly assessing someone is the first step in stopping the Halo Effect, but the problem with the Halo Effect is that we hardly ever are. You'll be able to judge something or someone more accurately if you can learn to do so without allowing your own mind to influence your decision.

A case study of the Halo Effect: You could also immediately associate someone who is overweight with other undesirable traits. "How did you grow so big?" "They must be slothful," The Halo Effect can make assumptions about someone based on just one glance at them, which is ugly and you don't necessarily do it on purpose.

2. Give second chances to your first impressions. Even though it's nearly impossible to avoid doing so when you've just met someone, try to be objective about your initial thoughts. Make an effort to provide evidence to support your sentiments for someone. Give someone a second opportunity if you are having trouble determining why you like or detest them.

3. You are prejudiced as well. Reflect you might also create the Halo Effect if you're lucky. In the event that you're not so fortunate, you can experience the Devil Effect. Consider your image carefully because it's simpler to criticize others than it is to recognize your own shortcomings.

A case study of the Halo Effect: Think about the reaction you received after asking a person you know well about their initial opinion of you.

4. Self-care is important.
Having good personal hygiene is crucial to fostering a favourable Halo Effect, regardless of weight, appearance, height, etc. Making a good first impression won't be aided by having oily hair, unpleasant body odour, or filthy nails.

Although it may seem obvious, you'd be shocked at how many people manage to attend a job interview while sporting a soiled shirt or oily hair.

5. The Halo Effect's grin

A smile conveys sympathy, friendliness, and empathy. According to studies, when you grin, the other person also begins to smile as a result.

If someone grins with a genuine, sincere smile, you're more likely to like them. Avoid putting on an overly forced smile like the Joker. You'll come across as false and unlikeable, and it will do you more harm than good.

6. Be logical

Being coherent, or staying true to your values, principles, preferences, and interests, is crucial for maximizing the Halo Effect. When you speak your mind and follow through on your commitments, you are being coherent. Your Halo Effect will be noticeably diminished if you project an incoherent image since the other person will perceive you as a cheater or liar and you run the risk of being judged by the Devil Effect.

An illustration of the Halo Effect is when a politician promises during the campaign to raise the minimum wage, but once in government, the wage is actually decreased.

7. Be mindful of your body language

More than 70% of what the other person experiences is communicated through non-verbal cues. Moving in a certain way, speaking in a certain tone, looking someone in the eyes or avoiding them, nodding, and other seemingly little body language clues reveal a lot more than you may imagine.

8. Pose inquiries to yourself.

Analyse yourself. Ask yourself honestly if your opinion would change if the person or thing you are judging had a different image before you make any decisions.

9. Avoid making generalizations, both negative and positive

Don't let other people's opinions influence you too much. Please only consider recommendations made by those who possess genuine industry knowledge. Consider their recommendations while making a decision if they have any power on the matter. You shouldn't take someone's word for truth if they don't have any relevant experience.

"No one has been talking to that new girl, so why would I?" is an example of the Halo Effect.

10. Become adept at using your instincts.

Balance is the most crucial aspect of life, to sum up. Don't doubt yourself or your instincts after reading this article since they might be accurate! Can you even begin to calculate how many friends, sights, and experiences you have lost out on all because of a single initial impression?